INDIAN
GODS, HEROES, AND MYTHOLOGY

BY TAMMY GAGNE

CONTENT CONSULTANT
Andrew Nicholson
Associate Professor of Asian & Asian American Studies
Stony Brook University

Core Library

An Imprint of Abdo Publishing
abdobooks.com

Cover image: Ganesha is an Indian deity often shown
with the head of an elephant.

abdocorelibrary.com

Printed in the United States of America, North Mankato, Minnesota
092018
012019

THIS BOOK CONTAINS
RECYCLED MATERIALS

Cover Photo: iStockphoto
Interior Photos: iStockphoto, 1, 16, 24–25, 43; Narinder Nanu/AFP/Getty Images, 4–5; Michael Nicholson/Corbis Historical/Getty Images, 9; Sohel Parvez Haque/iStockphoto, 11; Claudine Van Massenhove/Shutterstock Images, 12–13; Manjunath Kiran/AFP/Getty Images, 18–19, 45; Chantawute Chimwan/Shutterstock Images, 21; NASA, 28; Shutterstock Images, 30; Binod Joshi/AP Images, 32–33; Niranjan Shrestha/AP Images, 36; Nila Newsome/Shutterstock Images, 39; Santhosh Varghese/Shutterstock Images, 40

Editor: Marie Pearson
Series Designer: Ryan Gale

Library of Congress Control Number: 2018949774

Publisher's Cataloging-in-Publication Data

Names: Gagne, Tammy, author.
Title: Indian gods, heroes, and mythology / by Tammy Gagne.
Description: Minneapolis, Minnesota : Abdo Publishing, 2019 | Series: Gods, heroes, and mythology | Includes online resources and index.
Identifiers: ISBN 9781532117831 (lib. bdg.) | ISBN 9781532170690 (ebook)
Subjects: LCSH: Indic mythology--Juvenile literature. | Hinduism--Juvenile literature. | Heroes--Juvenile literature.
Classification: DDC 294.51--dc23

Special thanks to Silvia Nicholson for her valuable feedback on this book.

CONTENTS

THE ORIGINS OF INDIAN MYTHOLOGY

More than 2,000 years ago, a sage named Valmiki was walking along the Tamasa River in India when he came upon a pair of birds. As the male bird sang to the female, Valmiki stopped to take in the heartwarming moment. But it was interrupted when an arrow burst through the air. The weapon struck the male bird's chest. In an instant he fell to the ground. The female was heartbroken as her mate lay dying before her. Valmiki turned to see a hunter approaching with his bow in hand. He was outraged and cursed the hunter:

Hindus continue to honor Valmiki today.

You will find no rest for the long years of Eternity,

For you killed a bird in love and unsuspecting.

Valmiki could not forget the injustice of the bird's death. It inspired him to write an epic poem called the *Ramayana*. This long poem tells the story of a prince called Rama. Rama battles to rescue his wife, Sita, from an evil king called Ravana. The poem teaches important values and lessons.

In his poem, Valmiki also included descriptions of the gods and beliefs of the Hindu religion. Hinduism, one of the oldest religions of the world, can be traced as far back as 2500 BCE or perhaps even further. Its stories began in ancient Indian texts called the Vedas. Valmiki drew upon these ancient stories and added to them.

Today, Valmiki is known as a great poet of Indian literature. The stories he told in the *Ramayana* are a part of Indian mythology—a collection of myths, or stories, that are important to Indian culture. Like all myths, the stories in the *Ramayana* include magical or supernatural characters and events. They contain truths about life that more realistic-sounding stories cannot express. The stories are important to Hindus around the world.

ONE SOUL, MANY LIFETIMES

In Hindu belief, all living things experience a cycle of birth, death, and rebirth. Hindus believe that all beings live many times through reincarnation. After death, each soul is reincarnated, or reborn into a new body. Over the course of a lifetime, if a soul does good things, that soul has good karma. Souls with good karma will be rewarded when they are born into their next life. However, if a soul has done bad things, bad

THE VAITARANI

Indian mythology states that when people die, they cross the Vaitarani. This river separates the living from the dead. On the other side is a place called Pitriloka (pronounced pih-trih-LOE-kuh). There, people can meet their ancestors. Souls remain in Pitriloka until they are reborn into their next lifetimes. Each soul will cross the Vaitarani many times.

karma will cause the soul to be punished in the next life. To Hindus, this process explains why even good people sometimes suffer.

Reincarnation plays a role in many Indian stories. Many of the heroes of these tales are souls that are reborn into different lives. For instance, the god Vishnu was reborn ten times in different forms on Earth whenever he was needed to help restore goodness to humanity. Rama is the hero of Valmiki's epic *Ramayana*. He is also the seventh avatar, or form, of Vishnu. The god Krishna is another one of Vishnu's avatars. Vishnu, Rama, and Krishna all look different and lead different lives, but they share the same soul.

THE FOUR YUGAS

In Indian mythology, history is divided into four periods of time called yugas. The first was Krita Yuga. This yuga was a nearly perfect time. People were good and kind. They shared thoughts and ideas freely. They did not even need words to communicate. During this yuga,

AVATARS OF VISHNU

Each Indian god may have many different avatars. As Matsya, *left*, Vishnu lived as a fish. As Kurma, *center*, he was a tortoise. And as Varaha, *right*, he was a boar. Vishnu's other seven avatars were also completely different. What abilities would each of these forms have given Vishnu?

humans were the size of giants. They towered some 30 feet (9 m) tall.

Next came Treta Yuga. This period marked a change in humanity. People had become highly intelligent. But they were no longer as good. They had lost one-quarter of their truth. They were also shorter—approximately 20 feet (6 m) tall.

During the third era, the Dvapara Yuga, approximately one-half of truth had been lost.

People had become eviler. They cared more about power than spiritual knowledge. By the fourth era, Kali Yuga, people were filled with harmful emotions such as hatred. Kali Yuga is considered the darkest of the four yugas. This is the present yuga.

Time is measured differently in these yugas than people think of it today. Krita Yuga lasted 4,000 divine years. Each divine year is equal to 432,000 earthly years. Each yuga is shorter than the one before it. Treta Yuga lasted for 3,000 divine years. Dvapara lasted 2,000. Kali will last 1,000.

The stories of the yugas, gods, and heroes all play a part in Indian culture. Hindus look to these stories for

SHORTENED LIVES

In addition to being shorter in height, humans living during Kali Yuga have the shortest lifespans ever. They live only about 70 years. This is a far cry from the 4,000 or more years that people lived to during Krita Yuga. Some Hindus link this difference to the increasing darkness in the world over the four yugas.

Krishna was born in Dvapara Yuga. Hindus celebrate his birth on Janmashtami in August or September by dressing as the deity.

the many lessons they teach. Indian mythology lives on through the people who read and share these stories to this day.

INDIAN GODS AND GODDESSES

Hindu mythology includes many gods and goddesses. But some Hindus believe that all the gods are just different sides of one Highest Reality, known as Brahman. Brahman also exists in every person. It is the cause of everything—male and female, good and evil, and creation and destruction.

Brahma, Vishnu, and Shiva are all parts of Brahman. These three are important

Brahma, *left*, Shiva, *middle*, and Vishnu, *right*, are called the Trimurti.

13

BALANCING THE WORLD

In many Hindu stories, the god Brahma offers immortality to a human or demon. But the other gods limit the gift or take it away. The message of these stories is that only gods are supposed to be immortal. Human lives must end. The other gods limited Brahma so that his actions did not disrupt the cycle of life on Earth. They kept the world balanced.

gods in Hinduism. Brahma is the world's creator. However, some stories say Vishnu created Brahma. Many pictures of Brahma show him coming from Vishnu's navel. Vishnu became the world's protector. Many Hindus consider him to be the most important of the gods. Vishnu is most often seen in drawings as standing on a lotus flower or resting on a coiled serpent.

Shiva is known as a god of destruction. In his most destructive mood he is called Rudra. Rudra brings death and disease. At the same time, Shiva has great wisdom. The god's third eye, in the center of his forehead, represents wisdom. In some pictures he also wears a cobra necklace. It stands for his power over dangerous creatures. Some Hindus say Shiva, not Vishnu, created Brahma and the other gods.

IMPORTANT GODDESSES

The goddess Parvati is Shiva's wife. She brings balance to Shiva. When Shiva is disrespectful and behaves badly, Parvati shows her disapproval. Once she even leaves him. Parvati's rejection leads Shiva to be reborn into a more peaceful form. In one story, he becomes a sage named Durvasa. Shiva and Parvati have at least two sons. One of them is Ganesha, the god who removes obstacles and brings new beginnings.

SHAKTA GODDESS WORSHIP

Goddess worship is a popular tradition in Hindu culture. Called Shaktas, goddess worshippers view the goddess Devi as the supreme power of the universe. They place her above Vishnu and Shiva. Parvati is one of her many forms. As Parvati, Devi is one of Shiva's greatest teachers about the most important principles of Hinduism. Stories about her lessons to him are found in a collection of texts known as the Shakta Tantras.

Durga, *middle*, is often shown holding many weapons.

Goddesses play many roles. Durga, the warrior
goddess, is powerful. She is known for fighting against
evil. She vowed that she would only marry someone
who could defeat her in battle. The buffalo-demon
Mahisha fell deeply in love with Durga. When she
rejected his love, he gathered armies to try to kill her.
But she fought him and won, cutting off his head.

STRAIGHT TO THE
SOURCE

The Berkley Center for Religion, Peace & World Affairs website explains the roles that avatars play in Hindu mythology:

> *Avatars are an important aspect of Hinduism in defining the exchange between the human and divine realms. . . . Hinduism holds that gods can manifest at any time to help and guide the world. This open-ended view of human-divine exchange has allowed Hinduism to take a very tolerant approach to other religions by applying the concept of avatars to non-Hindu theologies; many Hindus believe that the Buddha, Jesus, and the Prophet Muhammad were all avatars, usually of Vishnu. In Hinduism . . . the images of gods often used in Hindu worship are often images of a god's avatar.*
>
> Source: "Avatar." *Berkley Center for Religion, Peace & World Affairs.* Georgetown University, n.d. Web. Accessed March 30, 2018.

Consider Your Audience
Review this passage closely. Consider how you would adapt it for a different audience, such as your parents or younger friends. Write a blog post conveying this same information so it makes sense for the new audience. How does your new approach differ from the original text, and why?

CREATURES OF INDIAN MYTHOLOGY

Hindu myths feature many animals. Some are avatars of gods and goddesses. Many have amazing abilities. The nagas are beings that take the form of snakes. These snakes are the 1,000 children of the god Kasyapa and goddess Kadru. Nagas inherited powers from their divine parents. They can appear as snakes, humans, or half-snake, half-human. Their venom makes them deadly to humans. But they can also be helpful.

Hindus honor naga deities by rubbing sacred turmeric paste on naga figurines.

19

In one tale, the naga king Takshaka rescues an Indian prince named Candrangada (pronounced chun-DRAHN-guh-duh). While taking part in a boat race, the prince nearly drowns. Takshaka's servants save his life. They carry him to the underworld. There he recovers with the help of Takshaka's many daughters.

In another story, Balarama, one of Vishnu's avatars, dies. His soul leaves his body in the form of a white snake. The serpent slithers out of the god's mouth. It heads to the afterlife. There Balarama is welcomed by the rest of the nagas.

PART HUMAN, PART ANIMAL

Many Hindu gods have animal features. Ganesha, for example, has the body of a human and the head of an elephant. Animal features are symbols for the gods' abilities. Ganesha is known as the god who removes all obstacles. His appearance suggests that he has the strength of an elephant, whose powerful strides clear a path through the thickest jungle.

In some depictions, Garuda, *bottom*, looks more human, and in others he looks more birdlike.

GARUDA, THE SUN EAGLE

The feared nagas had one mortal enemy. Garuda, the sun eagle, preyed on snakes. The rivalry between Garuda and the snakes began even before Garuda's birth. Garuda's mother—Vinata—and the nagas' mother—Kadru—were bitter enemies. So their children also became foes.

Garuda appears in many Indian stories. When Kadru kidnaps Vinata, Garuda frees her. He offers Kadru a pot of divine nectar in exchange for his mother. Garuda also appears in many stories as Vishnu's mount. The gods and goddesses ride many animals. Brahma rides seven swans. Durga often rides a lion or tiger.

BIG, BIGGER, AND BIGGEST

Some big fish feature in Hindu stories. Timin is among these large fish. A larger one is called Timin-gila. It is large enough to swallow whales whole. And even bigger than Timin-gila is Timin-gila-gila. This fish is large enough to eat the other giant fish.

FLYING HORSES

A Hindu story explains why the world has horses today. According to the myth, a special horse named Uccaihshravas (ooch-eye-SHRUV-us) was born from the ocean a long time ago. This creature had wings. A demon took the horse for his own mount. When the gods saw this unique creature, many became jealous. They wanted to ride an animal this magnificent themselves. The creator gods granted their wishes and created winged horses for the gods to ride. But not all the gods were happy with the result. One god, Daksha, disliked the winged creatures. He cursed the horses by removing their wings.

Horses appear in many Hindu myths. Like many other creatures, they are often used as symbols. They may stand for power, war, or the ocean. One of Vishnu's avatars is Hayagriva. This god has the head of a horse and the body of a human.

EXPLORE ONLINE

Chapter Three talks about the creatures of Hindu mythology. Visit the website below to read about an animal Hindus consider sacred—the cow. As you know, every source is different. Which details in the article are the same as in this chapter? What new information did you learn?

HOLY COW: HINDUISM'S SACRED ANIMAL

abdocorelibrary.com/indian-mythology

THE BEST-KNOWN HINDU STORIES

Some Hindu stories have been retold for thousands of years. The details may change, but the lessons remain the same. Some stories tell of the creation of the world. Before Brahma could create the world, the creator god had to be created himself. In some stories, Brahma is born from a golden egg. In other myths, he emerges from a lotus flower growing out of Vishnu's navel.

Brahma needed help with the task of creation. As he sat and thought, 20 new

Brahma has four heads: front, back, left, and right.

gods leapt from Brahma's mind. These gods, called the Prajapatis (prah-JAAH-puh-tees), included Vishnu and Shiva. Brahma himself is counted as one of the Prajapatis. Their work is found in many Hindu stories. Each time the world is destroyed, the Prajapatis recreate it.

The first universe they created lasted for just one day. But this first day was equal to 4 billion years as people now count them. At the end of the universe's first day, it was destroyed. The Prajapatis then recreated it for the first of many times.

SITA'S RESCUE

Valmiki's *Ramayana* tells of the capture and rescue of Rama's wife, Sita. The trouble began when King Dasharatha decided to pass his kingdom to Rama. One of the king's wives objected. She wanted her son Bharata to be king. So she forced Dasharatha to banish Rama to the forest for 14 years. Rama had done nothing wrong.

Rama warned Sita not to follow him into the forest. He knew dangerous demons lived there. But Sita refused to stay behind. She insisted that a wife's place is by the side of her husband. One demon in the forest was Surpanakha (shoor-PUH-nuh-kaah). She fell in love with Rama. But he rejected her. This angered Surpanakha. So she told her older brother Ravana about Sita's beauty. He kidnapped Sita and took her to a place called Lanka. Miles of ocean water separated Lanka

KARMA

The Hindu concept of karma brings positive effects to a person who has carried out good deeds in his or her lifetime. Likewise, a person's bad deeds have negative effects. But these effects are not always immediate or even quick. Hindus believe that karma is a process that may be carried out in future lifetimes. For instance, a person who does bad things in one lifetime may come back as a lowly animal in the next. Some Hindus believe that the gods themselves hand out karma to each soul. Others think of karma as an automatic result that does not involve the gods.

RAMA SETU
BRIDGE

The Rama Setu Bridge, *circled*, stretched from India to what is now Sri Lanka. Although the bridge itself is now largely underwater, many Hindus visit the site because of its religious significance. How do you think people may have used the bridge in the past?

INDIA

SRI LANKA

from India. Because Rama was a good man, he won the help of a monkey god named Hanuman. Together with his monkey army, Hanuman built an enormous bridge between India and Lanka. The Rama Setu Bridge made it possible for Rama to find his wife and defeat her captor.

THE STORY OF MATSYA

One of the best-known Indian stories is of Vishnu's fish avatar, known as Matsya. Near the end of one of the world's ages, Vishnu appeared in the form

TWO FLOOD STORIES

Stories of a great flood are found throughout the world. The story of Manu and the Christian tale of Noah's ark are two examples. The tales have much in common. Both Manu and Noah are described as honorable men. Each of them also has three sons. In the Hindu story, Vishnu helps Manu save his people from a great flood. He advises Manu to build a boat. He wants Manu to fill it with animals so the species do not die out. In the story from the Bible, God tells Noah to build the ark for the same reason. Both men save humanity. And both Manu's boat and Noah's ark end up in the mountains after the floods.

Sometimes Matsya is shown as half human, half fish. Other times, he is shown as all fish.

of a fish called Matsya. He was just a tiny fish when a man named Manu found him. But he kept growing. As the fish kept getting bigger, Manu kept moving him to larger bodies of water. Finally, Manu had to move Matsya to the ocean. There, Matsya became a gigantic fish with a large horn. Matsya revealed his true identity as the god Vishnu.

The fish-god warned Manu that a dreadful flood was coming. He told Manu to get a boat. Matsya then told Manu to place animals and plants in it to save them. Manu did as Matsya instructed. Next Matsya had Manu tie a rope to his horn and attach the boat to it. This allowed Matsya to pull the boat to safety during the storms and the flooding that followed. After the water finally receded, Manu thanked Vishnu for saving him. Vishnu then created a woman named Ida. She and Manu became the first man and woman of the world's next age.

FURTHER EVIDENCE

Chapter Four includes several of the most common Hindu stories. What is the main point of the chapter? What evidence was given to support that point? Visit the website below to learn more about Indian mythology. Choose a quote from one of the stories that relates to this chapter. Does this quote support the author's main point? Does it make a new point? Write a few sentences explaining how the quote you found relates to this chapter.

HINDU STORIES
abdocorelibrary.com/indian-mythology

INDIAN STORIES LIVE ON

Hinduism is the third largest religion in the world. It has more than 1 billion followers. Most live in India. Others live in Nepal, Bangladesh, and other countries. Only Christianity and Islam have more followers. But Hinduism's followers see it as much more than a religion. They often describe it as a way of life.

Hinduism differs from some other religions in the way it is practiced. Hindus do not attend a particular church or temple. They do not follow the teachings of a single person

One way Hindus practice their faith is by presenting offerings of food, flowers, and other items to specific gods.

OLD MEETS NEW

The superheroes on the pages of Indian comic books today may be older than they look. Some of these modern characters are actually the gods and goddesses of Hindu mythology. Comic books tell young people these ancient stories in new ways. One popular title is *Ramayan 3392 AD*. This comic book series retells the story of the *Ramayana* in a setting far in the future. Advanced technology gives the superheroes many of their special powers.

or book. So scholars cannot say exactly when Hinduism began. This does not bother most Hindus. They tend to care more about Hinduism's teachings than historical records.

Hindus believe that gods shared the most important stories with humans long ago. People then began retelling the stories to share their many lessons. The stories are still told by word of mouth and through books today. In this way, Hindu mythology remains a vital part of the Hindu religion and culture.

MISCONCEPTIONS

People often think of Hinduism as a polytheistic religion, or having many different gods. This is not necessarily true. There are many gods and goddesses. But many Hindus believe these gods are all aspects of one Higher Reality. For this reason, some scholars classify Hinduism as a monotheistic religion, or having one god. But not everyone agrees with that description, either. Some Hindus describe their faith as polytheistic. Some Hindus even call themselves atheists. They do not believe that a god created the universe, but they may still practice yoga or believe in reincarnation. Hinduism is so diverse that Hindus often feel free to choose the beliefs and practices that best suit them.

It is widely known that Hindus respect cows as sacred animals. Cows are often allowed to wander freely through Indian cities. People are not allowed to harm them. Because of this, some non-Hindus mistakenly think that Indians worship cows. This is not true. Rather, the cow is highly valued for its great importance in

agriculture throughout India. Cows provide milk and pull plows in the fields. They are honored for their hard work and their gentle nature. Another common misconception is that all Hindus are vegetarians. Hindus do believe that animals have souls. For these reasons, approximately one-third of Hindus do not eat meat. However, the majority do eat meat.

SECTS OF HINDUISM

Hindu followers can be divided into several smaller groups, or sects. Each sect has slightly different beliefs. For example, some followers are devoted to Vishnu. Others prefer to devote themselves to Shiva. Still others devote themselves to Devi, the Goddess. Some sects believe that Brahman is a concept that goes beyond any physical form. They seek to understand Brahman through spiritual study and meditation.

Many of the beliefs and practices of Hinduism were first introduced in the Vedas. The Vedas were texts

During Tihar Festival, which happens in October or November, Hindus honor cows as well as other animals.

THE HINDU PRACTICE OF YOGA

Yoga is popular in India and many other parts of the world today. This spiritual practice helps people focus their senses and minds. It helps people look inward to see the connection between mind and body. Yoga has deep roots in Hinduism. It is mentioned in many Hindu texts. In the *Bhagavad Gita*, Krishna links different types of yoga to action, concentration, devotion, and knowledge. For Hindus, the ultimate goal of yoga is something called moksha. Moksha is a state of unity with the divine. Hindus believe that the divine exists in every living thing. Once united with it, a person is released from the cycle of rebirth.

composed in Sanskrit, the ancient language of India. Epic poems such as the *Ramayana* add to these stories. Another famous epic poem is the *Mahabharata*, written in roughly 200 CE. The most famous part of the poem is a section called the *Bhagavad Gita*, or the *Gita*. The *Gita* is known throughout the world. It offers teachings about practices such as meditation and yoga.

In the West, most people practice yoga for physical health. But in Hinduism, the spiritual benefits of yoga are the true purpose.

Hindus today celebrate their faith in many ways, including festivals.

People today turn to Indian mythology for many reasons. These stories help guide many people in their faith. Others take moral lessons from the myths. As with Hinduism itself, the stories mean different things to different people. But the lessons learned are valuable to each person.

STRAIGHT TO THE
SOURCE

George M. Williams, an author and professor of religious studies, explained that people do not have to believe everything about a myth to learn from it:

> *A Hindu does not have to "believe in" the details of the myths. . . . A Hindu can participate in the mythic meaning of a tradition simply by identifying with the myth's ability to help locate oneself within the community's worldview. . . . Outsiders will hear or read these myths and find them strange and even "untrue." . . . For the insider, the myths will be validated simply in the experience of belonging to a community. For the outsider, the same myths will be objects outside of one's experience. However, even the outsider can see universal themes—mythology's timeless contributions to human reflection.*

> Source: George M. Williams. *Handbook of Hindu Mythology.* Santa Barbara, CA: ABC-CLIO, 2003. Google Books. 2. Web. Accessed March 30, 2018.

What's the Big Idea?
Take a closer look at the passage. What is the main idea? Identify two or three pieces of evidence the author has included. In a few sentences, describe how Williams uses this evidence to support his main point.

FAST FACTS

Gods and Goddesses

- All the gods can be seen as part of one Higher Reality called Brahman.

- Brahma is the creator of the world.

- Durga, the warrior goddess, fights evil.

- Parvati is a form of the goddess Devi. As Shiva's wife, she balances Shiva's power. Their son is Ganesha.

- Shiva is the world's destroyer and re-creator.

- Vishnu is the protector of the world. Some Hindus believe he created Brahma.

Creatures

- Garuda is the sun eagle. An enemy of the nagas, he uses them as food.

- The nagas are serpents with supernatural powers.

- Uccaihshravas, a mythical horse with wings, was the ancestor of horses on earth.

Stories

- The creation myth tells the story of how Brahma made the world and everything in it.

- The story of Sita's rescue tells how Rama rescued Sita from the island of Lanka after she was kidnapped.

- The myth of Matsya tells the story of how the fish-god, Matsya, helped Manu save humanity after a great flood.

STOP AND
THINK

Tell the Tale

Chapter One of this book retells a legend about the Indian poet Valmiki. Indian tales have been retold many times by many people. Using what you remember about the story, retell it in your own words to a classmate or other friend. How much detail do you remember?

Dig Deeper

After reading this book, what questions do you still have about Indian mythology? With an adult's help, find a few reliable sources that will help you answer these questions. Write a paragraph about what you learned.

Surprise Me

Chapter Three talks about animals and other creatures that are part of Indian mythology. After reading this book, what facts about these creatures surprised you the most? Write a few sentences about each fact. Why did you find these details surprising?

You Are There

This book talks about several well-known Indian myths. Imagine that you witnessed one of these stories yourself. Write a letter home telling your family and friends about your experience. Be sure to add plenty of details.

GLOSSARY

atheist
a person who does not believe in the existence of a god or gods

karma
a person's good or bad actions, which are destined to be either rewarded or punished in the next lifetime

meditation
in Hinduism, practices such as chanting sacred words and reflecting on teachings that focus the mind, leading to a better understanding of the divine

mount
the animal someone rides

navel
the spot on the abdomen where the umbilical cord was attached

reincarnation
the process of being born into a new lifetime following death

sect
a group within a religion that has some different beliefs than other groups

supernatural
beings and events that do not follow the laws of nature

validate
to confirm or back up

yoga
a practice that involves meditation, breath control, and body postures for the health of mind and body

ONLINE RESOURCES

To learn more about Indian gods, heroes, and mythology, visit our free resource websites below.

Core Library CONNECTION
FREE! COMMON CORE MULTIMEDIA RESOURCES

Visit **abdocorelibrary.com** for free Common Core resources for teachers and students, including vetted activities, multimedia, and booklinks, for deeper subject comprehension.

Booklinks NONFICTION NETWORK
FREE! ONLINE NONFICTION RESOURCES

Visit **abdobooklinks.com** for free additional online weblinks for further learning. These links are routinely monitored and updated to provide the most current information available.

LEARN MORE

Pattanaik, Devdutt. *Pashu: Animal Tales from Hindu Mythology*. Gurgaon, Haryana, India: Puffin, 2014.

Sperling, Vatsala. *Arjuna: The Gentle Warrior*. Rochester, VT: Bear Cub, 2017.

INDEX

About the Author

Tammy Gagne has written dozens of books for both adults and children. Her recent titles include *Women in Engineering* and *Exploring the Southwest*. She lives in northern New England with her husband, son, and pets.